he Ultimate Self-Teaching Method!

Level One
Song
Book

Play
Accordion
Today! Songbook

Featuring 10 All-Time Favorites!

Arranged by Gary Meisner

Recorded and produced by
Jim Reith at BeatHouse Music,
Milwaukee, WI

Stan Fomin, Audio Arrangements
Gary Meisner, Accordion

ISBN 978-1-4584-1841-8

7777 W. BLUEMOUND RD. P.O. BOX 13819 MILWAUKEE, WI 53213

E-Z Play® Today Music Notation
© 1975 by HAL LEONARD CORPORATION

Visit Hal Leonard Online at
www.halleonard.com

Introduction

Welcome to the *Play Accordion Today! Songbook*. This book includes ten all-time favorite songs, and is intended for the beginning to intermediate accordion player.

The arrangements in this book are carefully correlated with the skills introduced in *Play Accordion Today! – Level One*. Refer to the table of contents to see where each song fits within the method and to help you determine when you're ready to play it.

About the CD

A full-band recording of every song in this book is included on the CD, so you can hear how it sounds and play along when you're ready. Each song is preceded by count-off "clicks" to indicate the tempo and meter.

The CD is playable on any CD player, and is also enhanced so Mac and PC users can adjust the recording to any tempo without changing the pitch! For the latest Amazing Slow Downer software and installation instructions, go to **www.halleonard.com/ASD.**

Contents

Gentle on My Mind

Words and Music by
JOHN HARTFORD

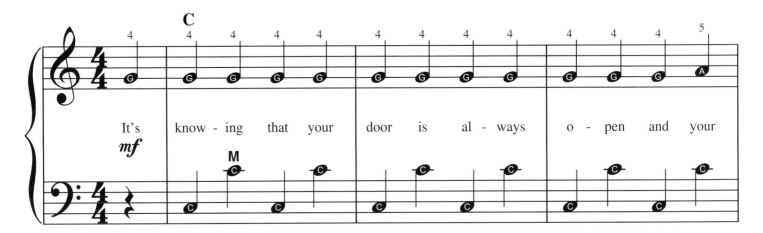

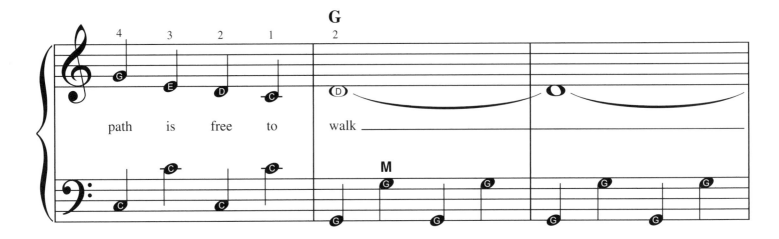

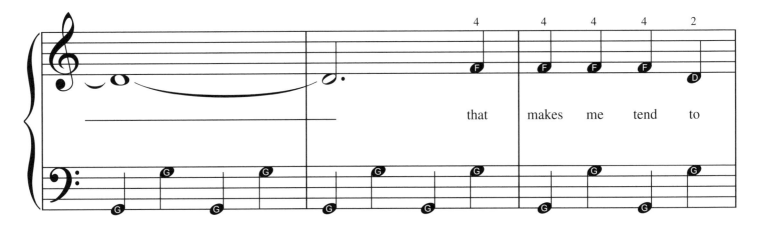

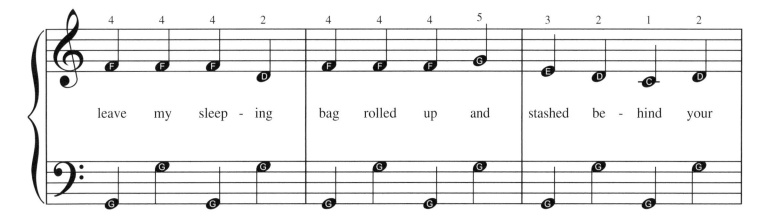

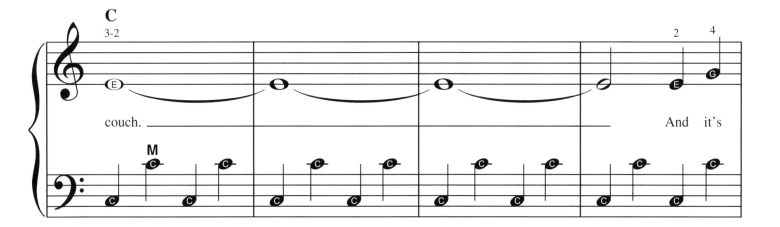

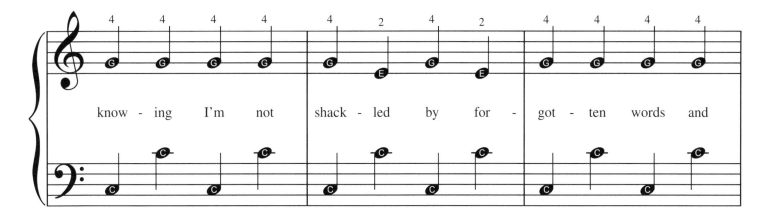

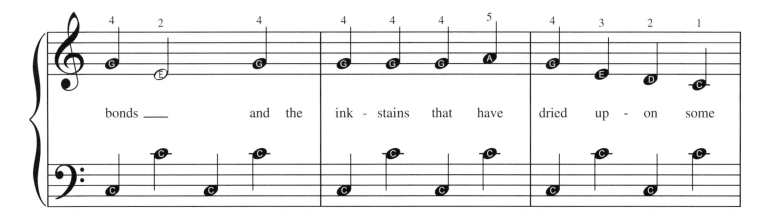

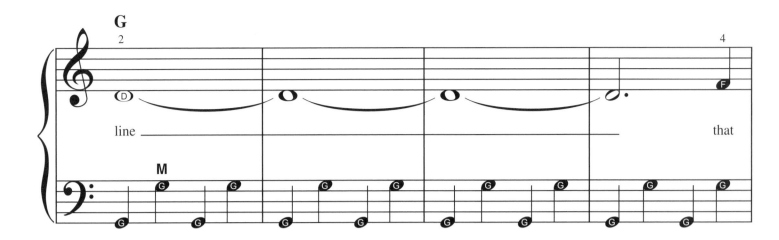

G

line _____ that

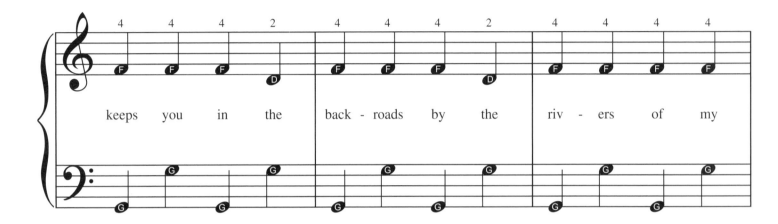

keeps you in the back - roads by the riv - ers of my

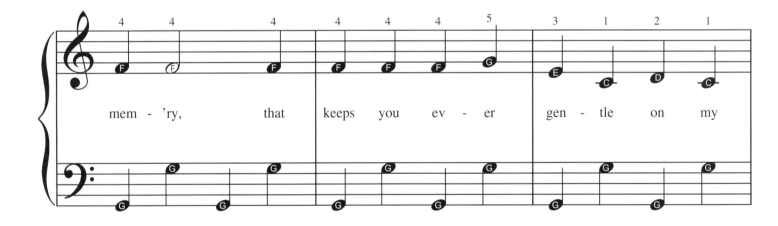

mem - 'ry, that keeps you ev - er gen - tle on my

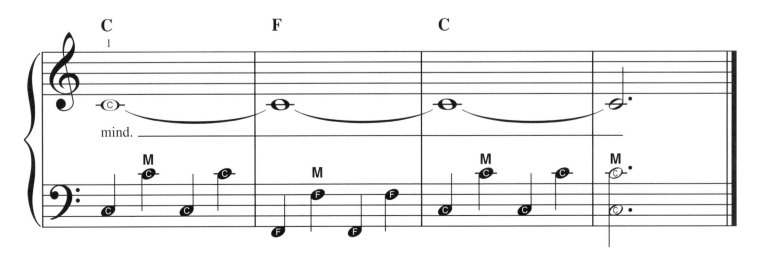

C   **F**   **C**

mind. _____

(Put Another Nickel In)
Music! Music! Music!

Words and Music by STEPHAN WEISS
and BERNIE BAUM

Moderately

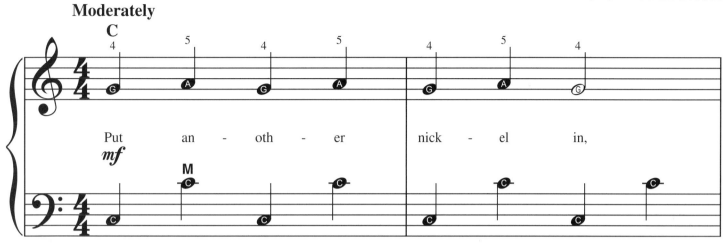

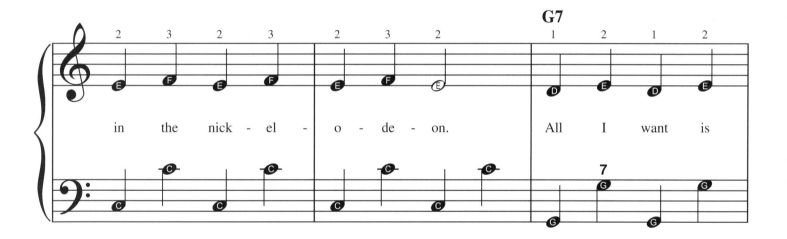

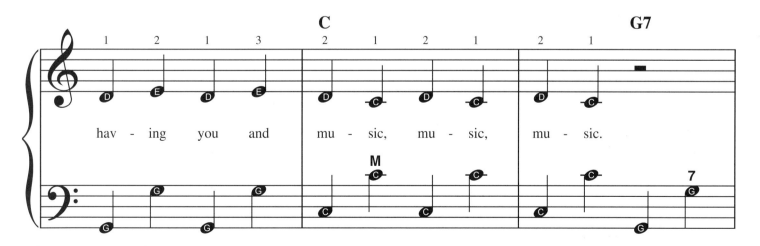

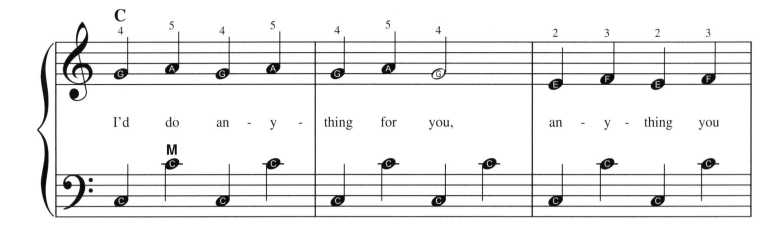

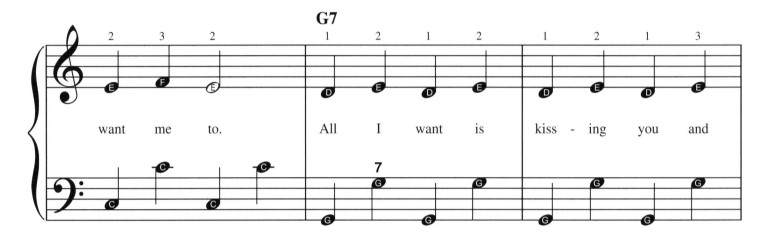

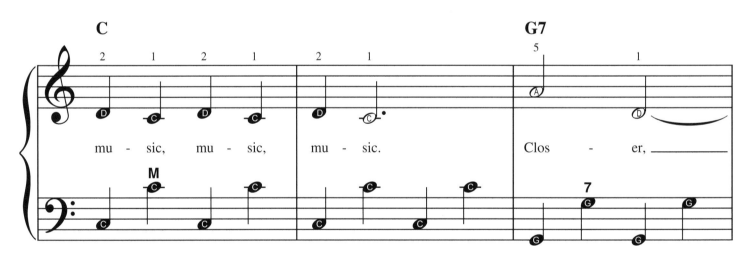

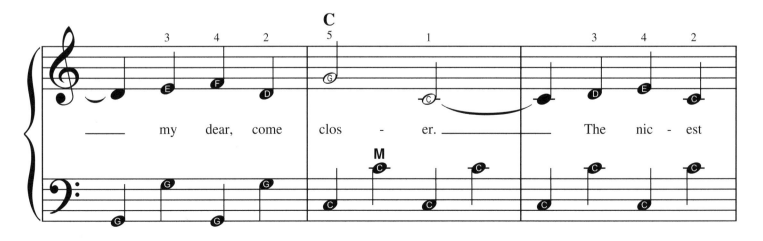

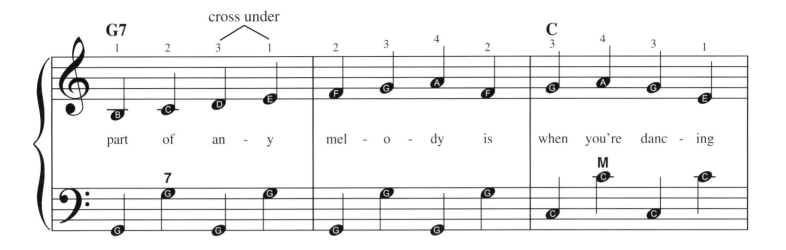

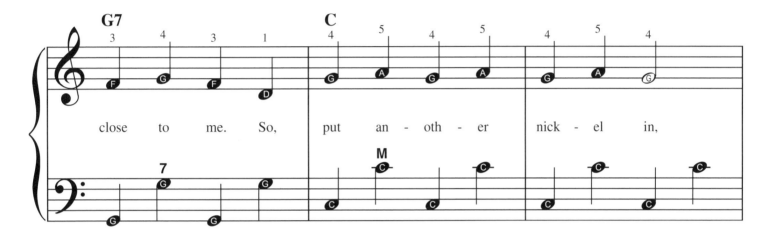

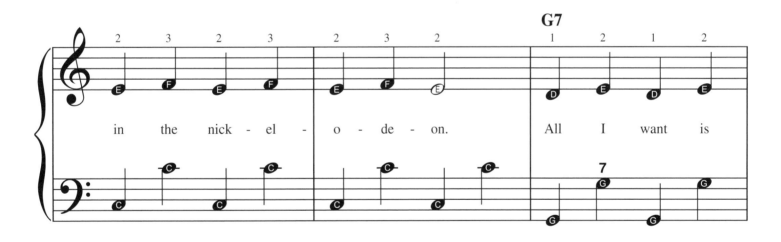

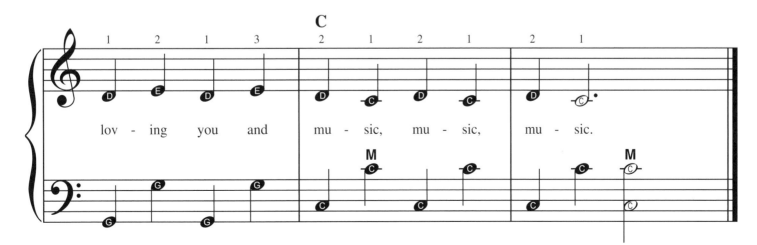

Too Fat Polka
(She's Too Fat for Me)

Words and Music by ROSS MacLEAN
and ARTHUR RICHARDSON

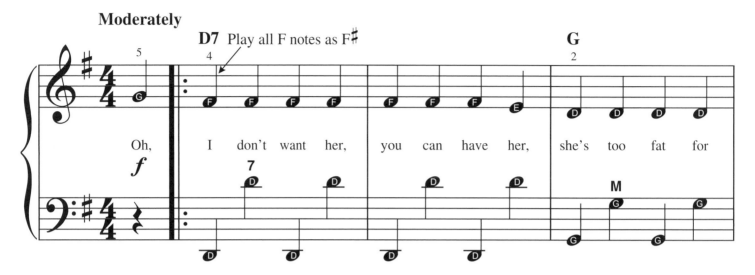

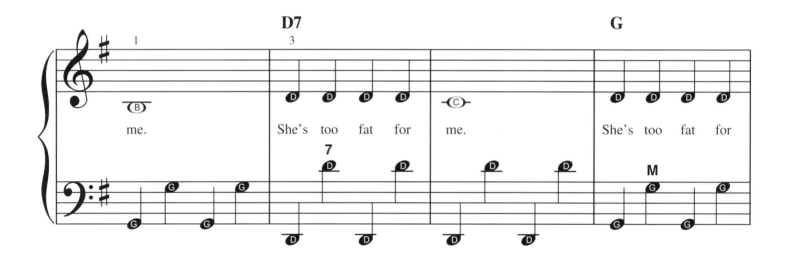

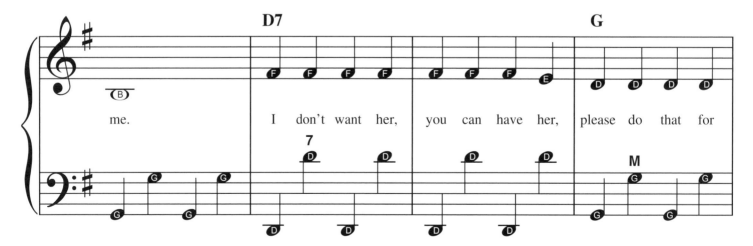

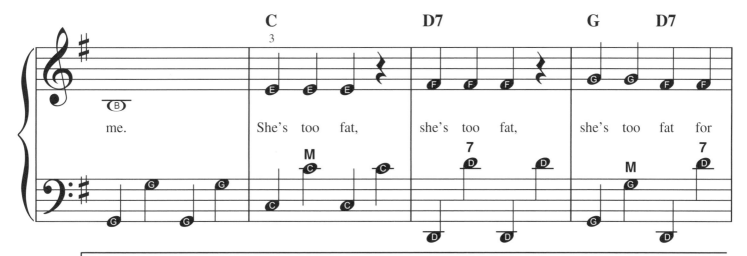

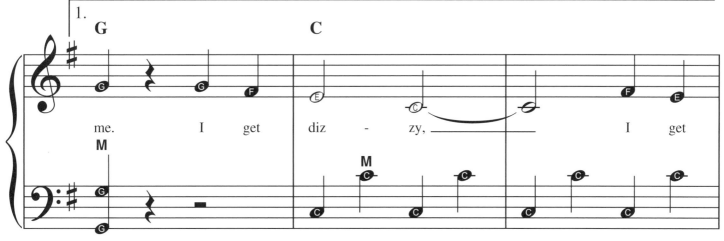

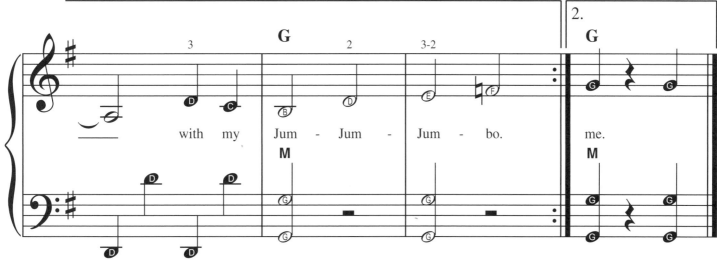

Supercalifragilisticexpialidocious

from Walt Disney's MARY POPPINS

Words and Music by RICHARD M. SHERMAN
and ROBERT B. SHERMAN

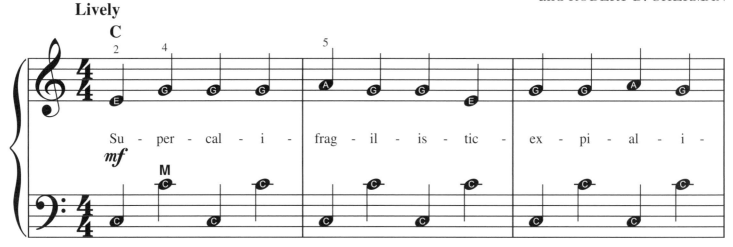

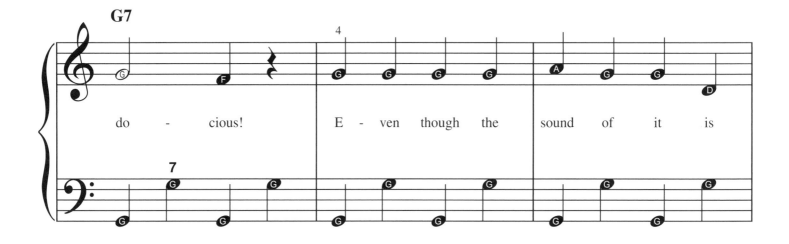

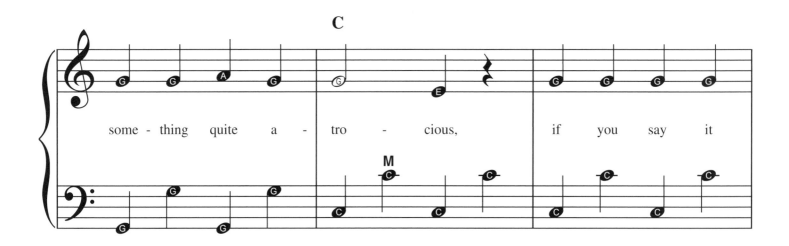

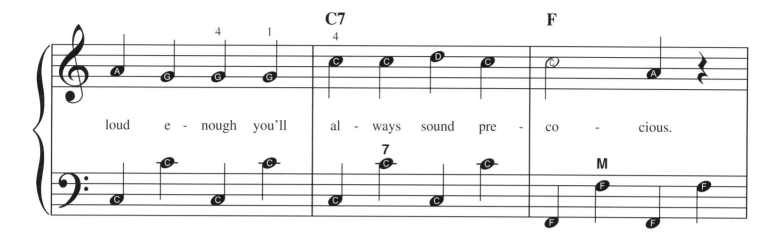

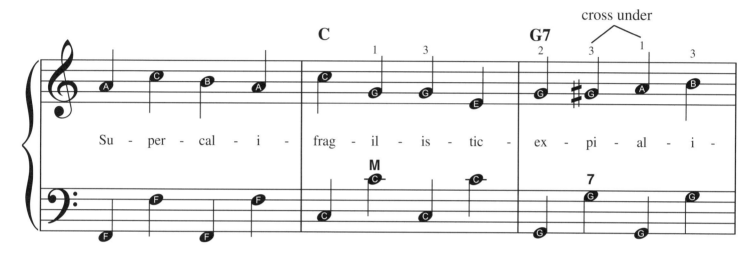

(This page is left intentionally blank to eliminate a page turn.)

Your Cheatin' Heart

Words and Music by
HANK WILLIAMS

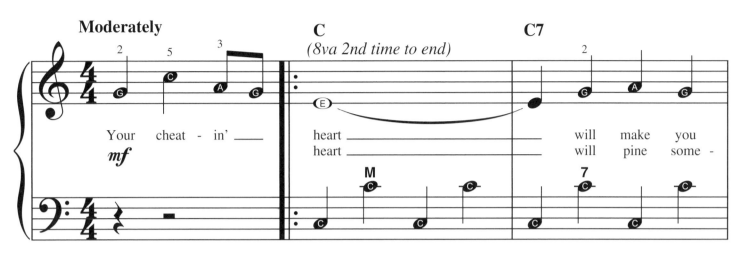

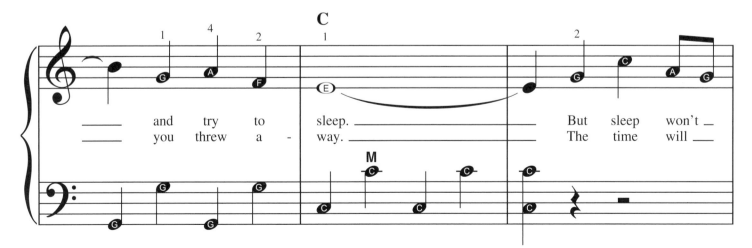

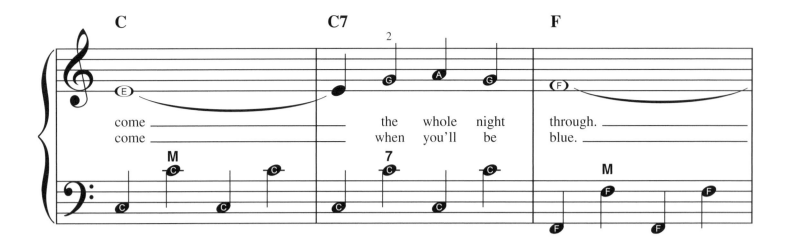

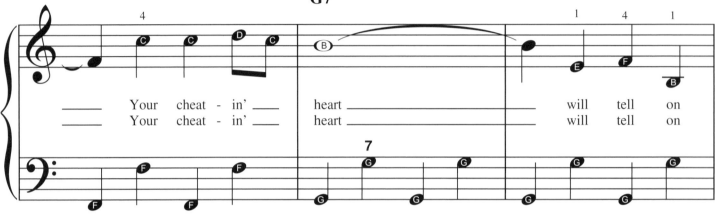

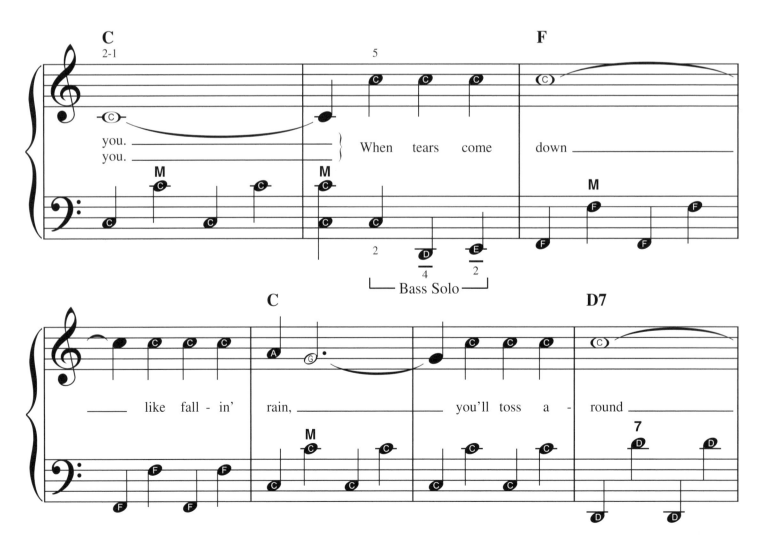

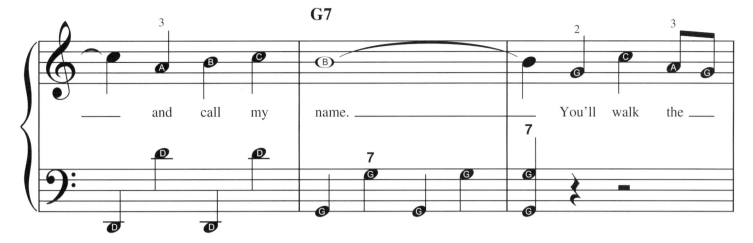

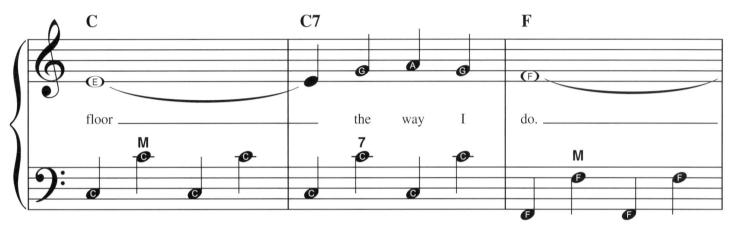

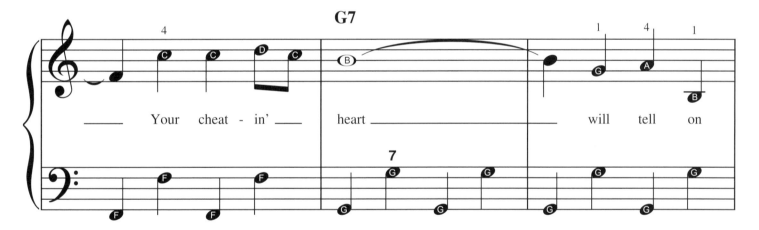

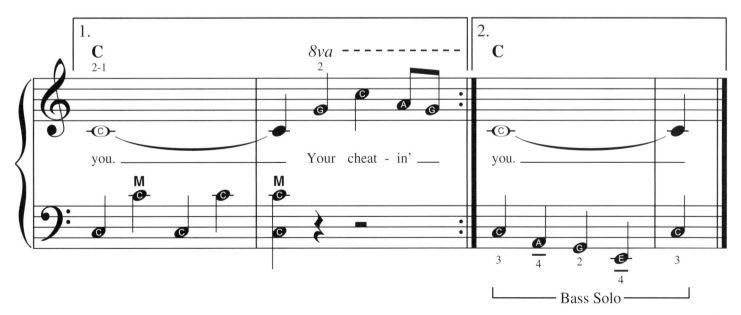

The Ballad of Davy Crockett

from Walt Disney's DAVY CROCKETT

Words by TOM BLACKBURN
Music by GEORGE BRUNS

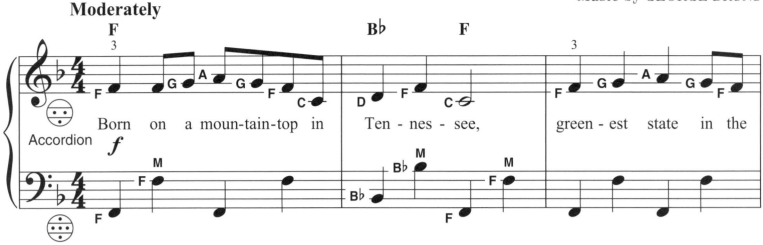

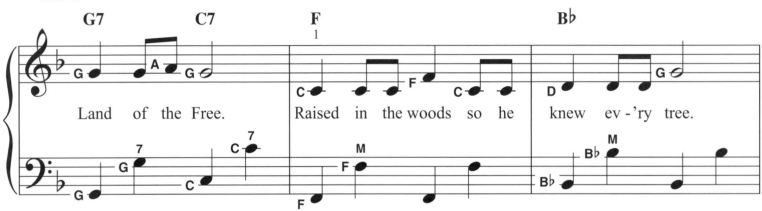

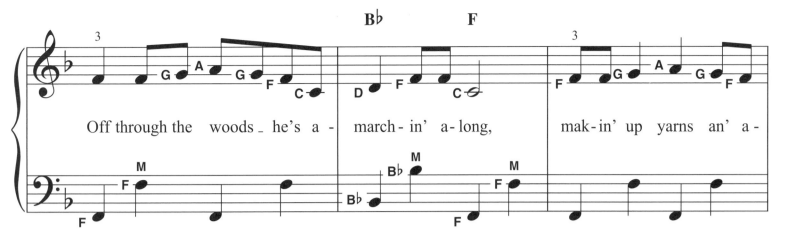

Off through the woods he's a- march-in' a-long, mak-in' up yarns an' a-

sing-in' a song. Itch-in' for fight-in' an' right-in' a wrong, he's

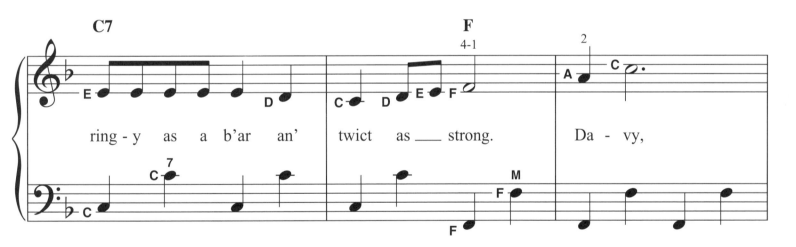

ring-y as a b'ar an' twict as ___ strong. Da-vy,

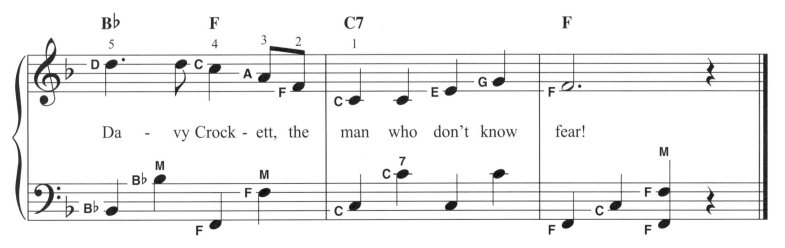

Da - vy Crock-ett, the man who don't know fear!

Can't Help Falling in Love

Words and Music by GEORGE DAVID WEISS,
HUGO PERETTI and LUIGI CREATORE

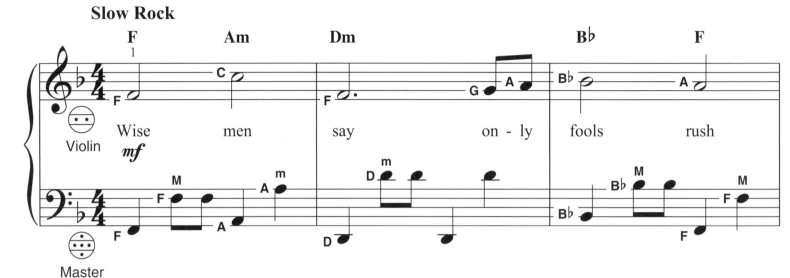

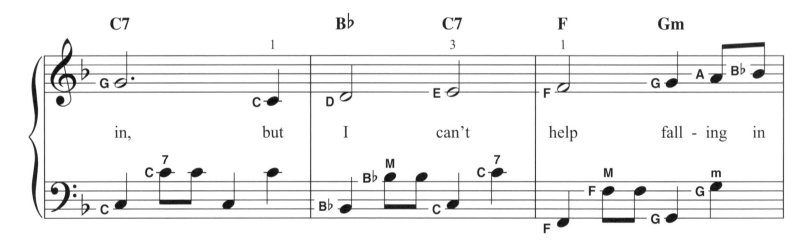

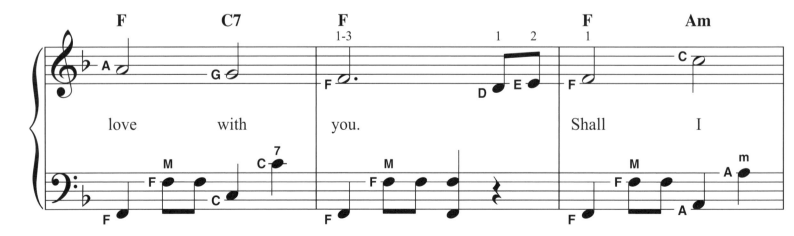

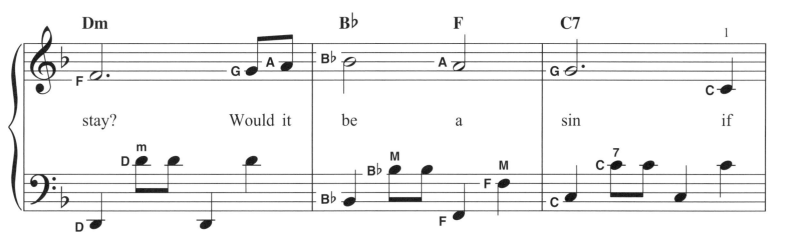

stay?   Would it   be   a   sin   if

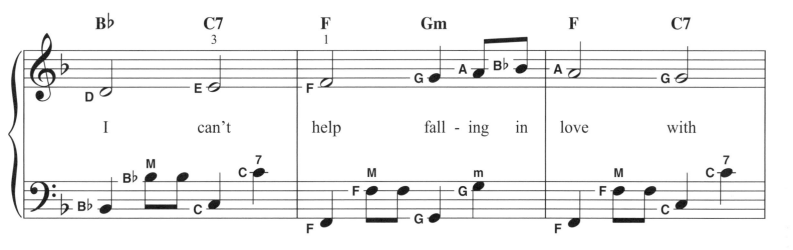

I   can't   help   fall - ing   in   love   with

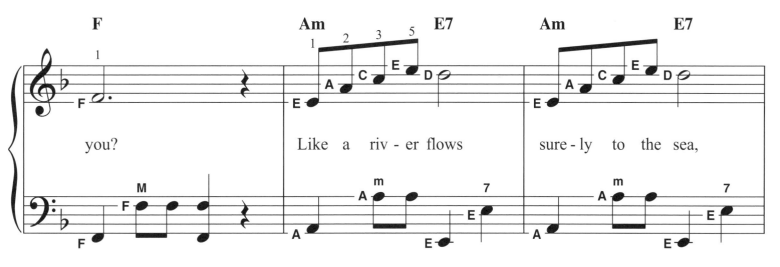

you?   Like   a   riv - er flows   sure - ly   to   the   sea,

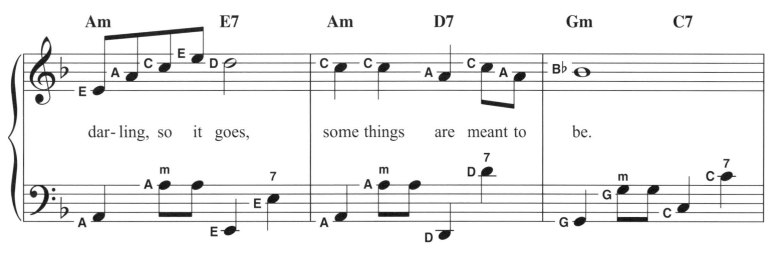

dar - ling, so   it   goes,   some things   are   meant to   be.

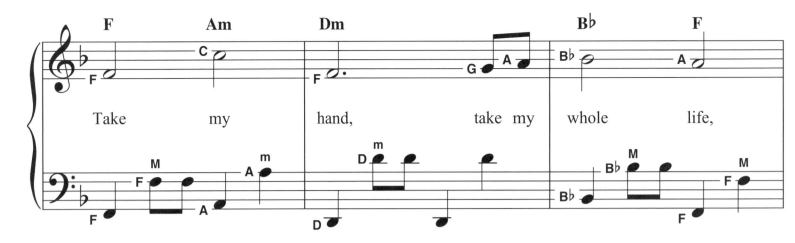

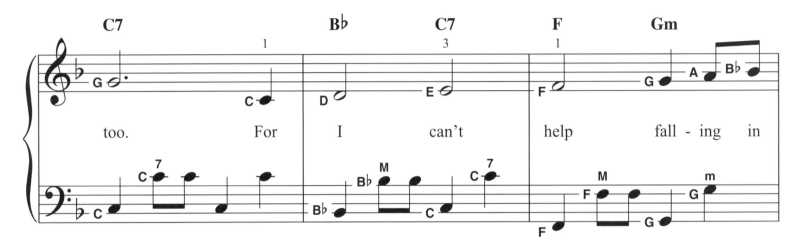

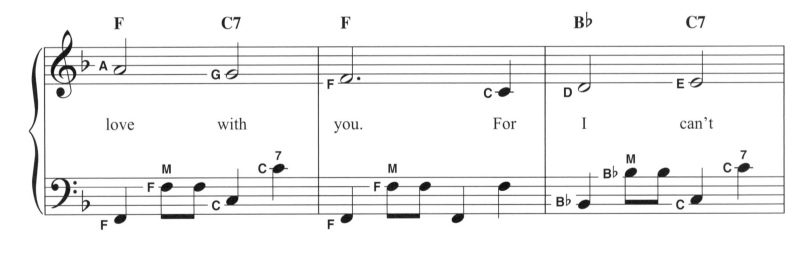

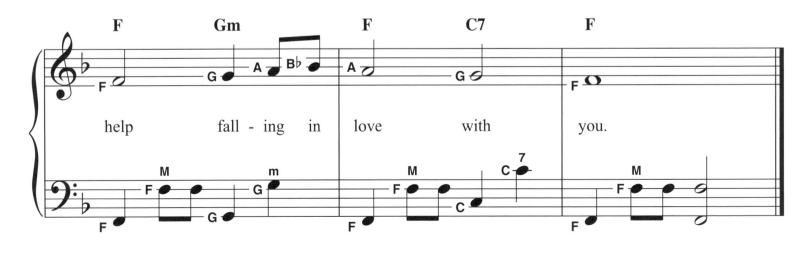

(This page is left intentionally blank to eliminate a page turn.)

Snowbird

Words and Music by
GENE MacLELLAN

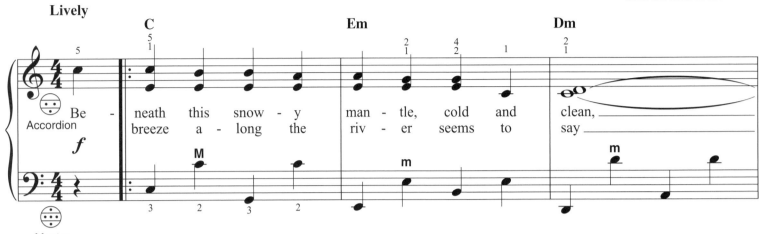

Be - neath this snow - y man - tle, cold and clean,
breeze a - long the riv - er seems to say

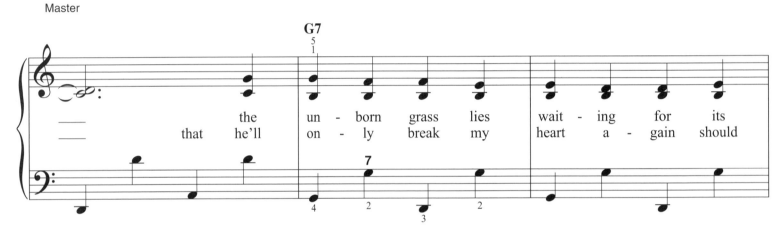

the un - born grass lies wait - ing for its
that he'll on - ly break my heart a - gain should

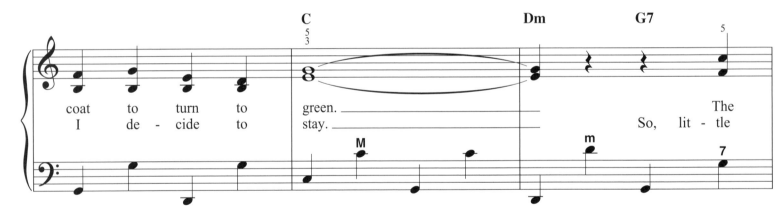

coat to turn to green.
I de - cide to stay. The
So, lit - tle

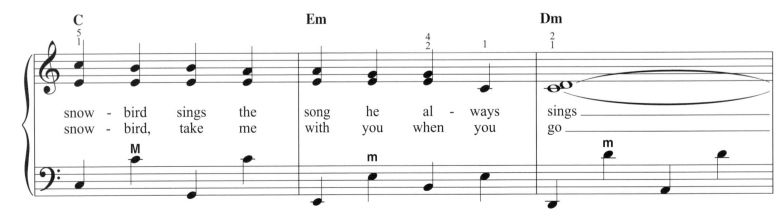

snow - bird sings the song he al - ways sings
snow - bird, take me with you when you go

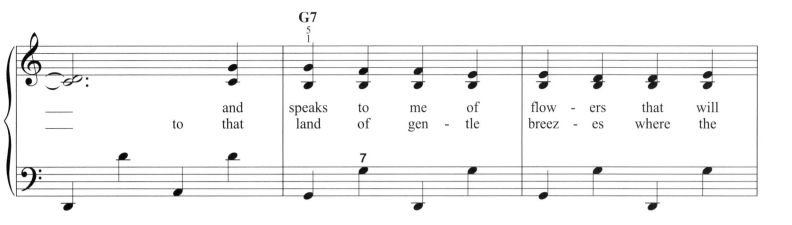

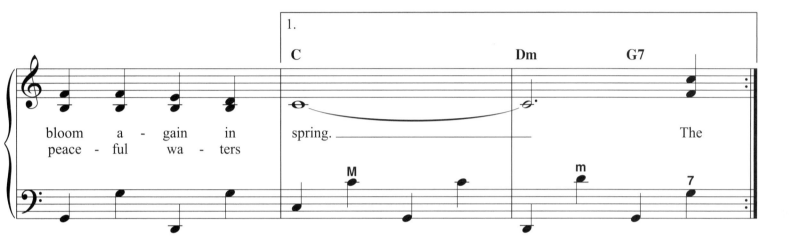

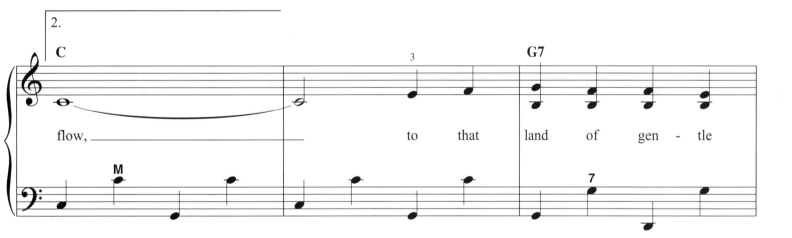

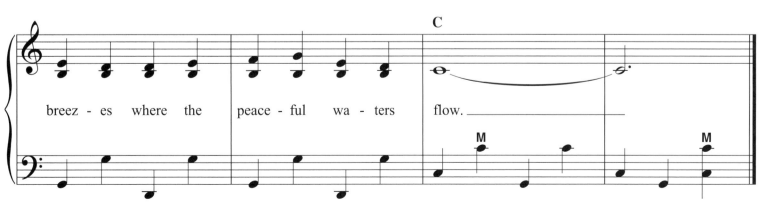

Tuxedo Junction

Track 9

Words by BUDDY FEYNE
Music by ERSKINE HAWKINS,
WILLIAM JOHNSON and JULIAN DASH

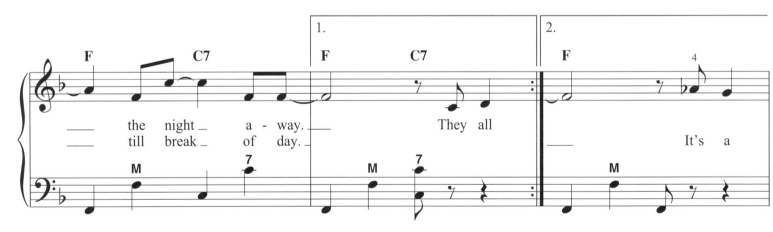

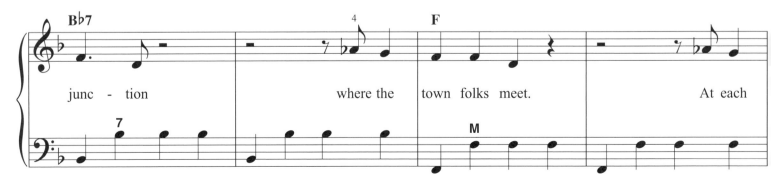

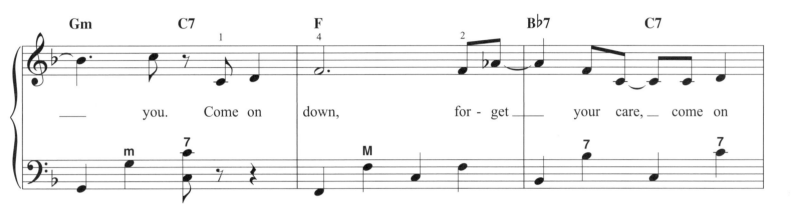

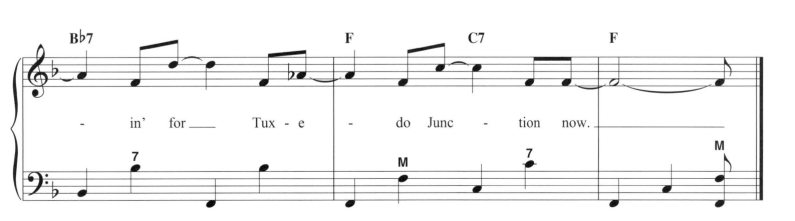

The Rainbow Connection

from THE MUPPET MOVIE

Track 10

Words and Music by PAUL WILLIAMS
and KENNETH L. ASCHER

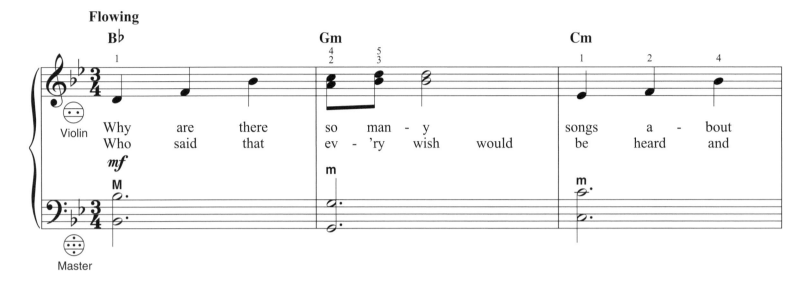

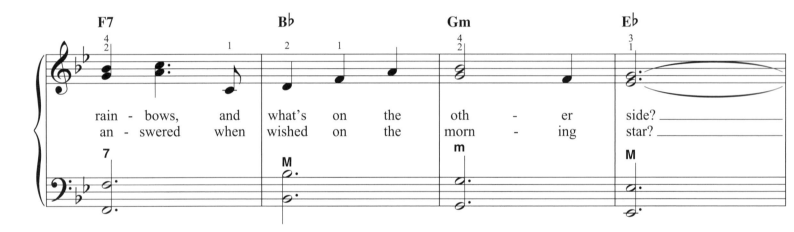

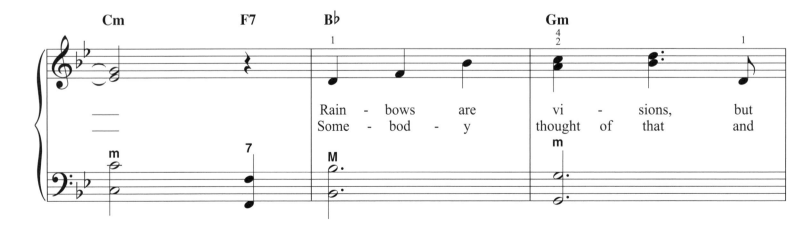

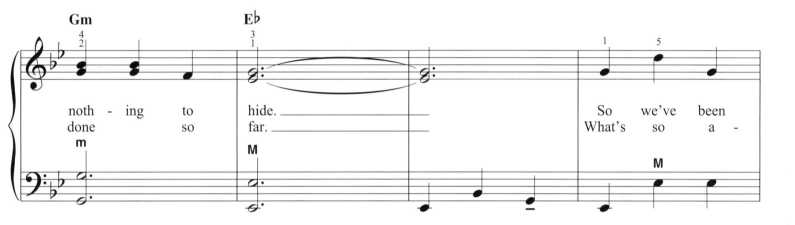

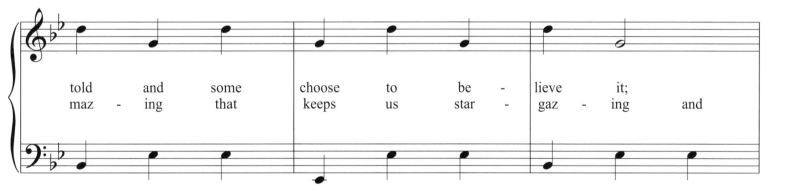

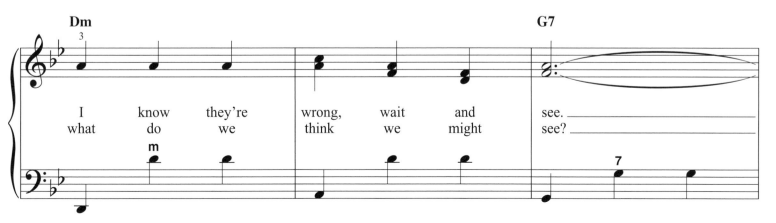

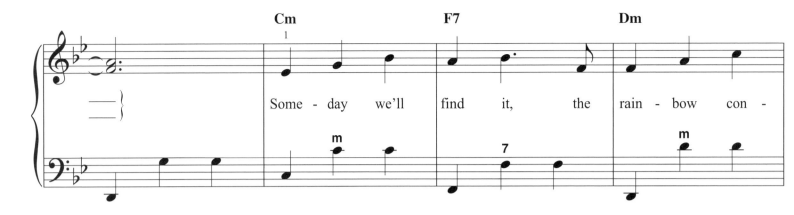

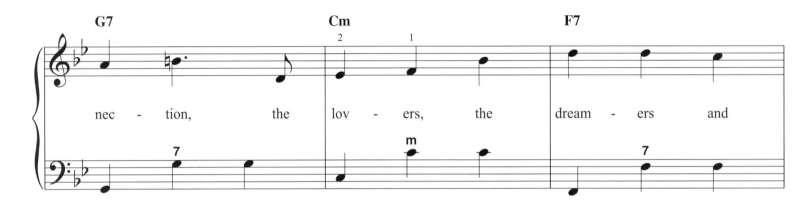

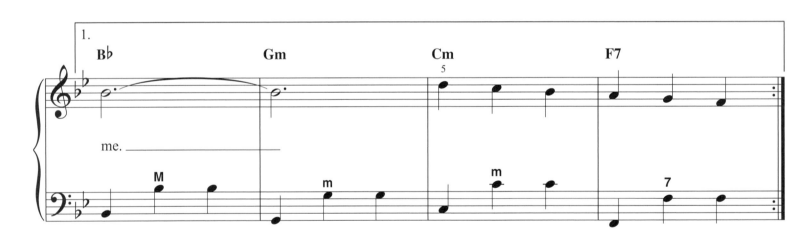

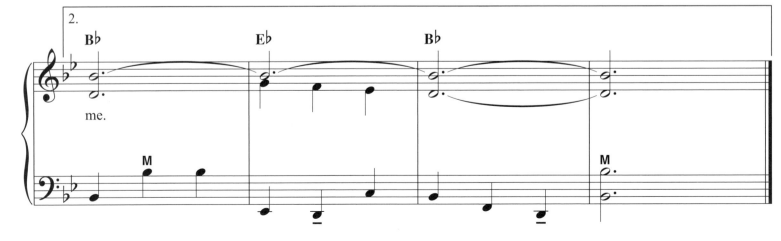

A COLLECTION OF ALL-TIME FAVORITES FOR ACCORDION

ACCORDION FAVORITES
arr. Gary Meisner

16 all-time favorites, arranged for accordion, including: Can't Smile Without You • Could I Have This Dance • Endless Love • Memory • Sunrise, Sunset • I.O.U. • and more.
00359012 ....$10.95

ALL-TIME FAVORITES FOR ACCORDION
arr. Gary Meisner

20 must-know standards arranged for accordions. Includes: Ain't Misbehavin' • Autumn Leaves • Crazy • Hello, Dolly! • Hey, Good Lookin' • Moon River • Speak Softly, Love • Unchained Melody • The Way We Were • Zip-A-Dee-Doo-Dah • and more.
00311088 ....$10.95

THE BEATLES GREATEST HITS FOR ACCORDION

15 of the Beatles greatest hits arranged for accordion. Includes: Lucy in the Sky with Diamonds • A Hard Day's Night • Yellow Submarine • All My Loving • Yesterday • Michelle • Hey Jude • more.
00359121 ....$12.99

BROADWAY FAVORITES
arr. Ken Kotwitz

A collection of 17 wonderful show songs, including: Don't Cry for Me Argentina • Getting to Know You • If I Were a Rich Man • Oklahoma • People Will Say We're in Love • We Kiss in a Shadow.
00490157 ....$9.95

CHRISTMAS SONGS FOR ACCORDION

17 holiday hits, including: The Chipmunk Song • Frosty the Snow Man • A Holly Jolly Christmas • Jingle-Bell Rock • Pretty Paper • Rudolph the Red-Nosed Reindeer.
00359477 ....$8.99

CONTEMPORARY HITS FOR ACCORDION
arr. Gary Meisner

15 songs, including: I Left My Heart in San Francisco • Just the Way You Are • Longer • September Morn • Somewhere Out There • Through the Years • and more.
00359491 ....$9.95

DISNEY MOVIE FAVORITES

Students will love playing these 12 songs from the Disney favorites *Aladdin, Beauty and the Beast*, and *The Little Mermaid*. Songs include: Under the Sea • Be Our Guest • A Whole New World • and more!
00311632 ....$9.95

ITALIAN SONGS FOR ACCORDION
arr. Gary Meisner

17 favorite Italian standards arranged for accordion, including: Carnival of Venice • Ciribiribin • Come Back to Sorrento • Funiculi, Funicula • La donna è mobile • La Spagnola • 'O Sole Mio • Santa Lucia • Tarantella • and more.
00311089 ....$9.95

LATIN FAVORITES FOR ACCORDION
arr. Gary Meisner

20 Latin favorites, including: Bésame Mucho (Kiss Me Much) • The Girl from Ipanema • How Insensitive (Insensatez) • Perfidia • Spanish Eyes • So Nice (Summer Samba) • and more.
00310932 ....$10.99

THE SONGS OF ANDREW LLOYD WEBBER FOR ACCORDION

10 of his best, including: All I Ask of You • Any Dream Will Do • As If We Never Said Goodbye • I Don't Know How to Love Him • Love Changes Everything • The Music of the Night • Old Deuteronomy • Think of Me • Unexpected Song • With One Look.
00310152 ....$10.95

POLKA FAVORITES
arr. Kenny Kotwitz

An exciting new collection of 16 songs, including: Beer Barrel Polka • Liechtensteiner Polka • My Melody of Love • Paloma Blanca • Pennsylvania Polka • Too Fat Polka • and more.
00311573 ....$10.95

WALTZ FAVORITES
arr. Kenny Kotwitz

Accordion arrangements of 17 classic waltzes, including: Alice Blue Gown • I Love You Truly • I Wonder Who's Kissing Her Now • I'll Be with You in Apple Blossom Time • Let Me Call You Sweetheart • Let the Rest of the World Go By • My Buddy • and more.
00310576 ....$9.95

LAWRENCE WELK'S POLKA FOLIO

More than 50 famous polkas, schottisches and waltzes arranged for piano and accordion, including: Blue Eyes • Budweiser Polka • Clarinet Polka • Cuckoo Polka • The Dove Polka • Draw One Polka • Gypsy Polka • Helena Polka • International Waltzes • Let's Have Another One • Schnitzelbank • Shuffle Schottische • Squeeze Box Polka • Waldteuful Waltzes • and more.
00123218 ....$10.95

FOR MORE INFORMATION,
SEE YOUR LOCAL MUSIC DEALER,
OR WRITE TO:

HAL•LEONARD®
CORPORATION
7777 W. BLUEMOUND RD. P.O. BOX 13819
MILWAUKEE, WISCONSIN 53213

Visit Hal Leonard Online at **www.halleonard.com**

PLAY TODAY® SERIES

THE ULTIMATE SELF-TEACHING SERIES!

How many times have you said: "I wish I would've learned to play guitar... piano... saxophone..." Well, it's time to do something about it. The revolutionary *Play Today!* Series from Hal Leonard will get you doing what you've always wanted to do: make music. Best of all, with these book/CD packs you can listen and learn at your own pace, in the comfort of your own home!

This method can be used by students who want to teach themselves or by teachers for private or group instruction. It is a complete guide to the basics, designed to offer quality instruction in the book and on the CD, terrific songs, and a professional-quality CD with tons of full-demo tracks and audio instruction. Each book includes over 70 great songs and examples!

Play Guitar Today! DVD · INCLUDES TAB
00696100 Level 1 Book/CD Pack..$9.95
00696101 Level 2 Book/CD Pack..$9.95
00320353 DVD $14.95
00696102 Songbook Book/CD Pack....................................$12.95
00699544 Beginner's Pack – Level 1 Book/CD & DVD $19.95
00842055 Play Today Plus Book/CD Pack............................$14.95

Play Bass Today! DVD · INCLUDES TAB
00842020 Level 1 Book/CD Pack..$9.95
00842036 Level 2 Book/CD Pack..$9.95
00320356 DVD $14.95
00842037 Songbook Book/CD Pack....................................$12.95
00699552 Beginner's Pack – Level 1 Book/CD & DVD $19.95
00698997 Play Today Plus Book/CD Pack............................$14.95

Play Drums Today! DVD
00842021 Level 1 Book/CD Pack..$9.95
00842038 Level 2 Book/CD Pack..$9.95
00320355 DVD $14.95
00842039 Songbook Book/CD Pack....................................$12.95
00699551 Beginner's Pack – Level 1 Book/CD & DVD $19.95
00699001 Play Today Plus Book/CD Pack............................$14.95

Play Piano Today! DVD
00842019 Level 1 Book/CD Pack..$9.95
00842040 Level 2 Book/CD Pack..$9.95
00320354 DVD $14.95
00842041 Songbook Book/CD Pack....................................$12.95
00699545 Beginner's Pack – Level 1 Book/CD & DVD $19.95
00699044 Play Today Plus Book/CD Pack............................$14.95

Sing Today!
00699761 Level 1 Book/CD Pack..$9.95

Play Ukulele Today!
00699638 Level 1 Book/CD Pack..$9.95
00699655 Play Today Plus Book/CD Pack............................$9.95

Play Alto Sax Today! DVD
00842049 Level 1 Book/CD Pack..$9.95
00842050 Level 2 Book/CD Pack..$9.95
00320359 DVD $14.95
00842051 Songbook Book/CD Pack....................................$12.95
00699555 Beginner's Pack – Level 1 Book/CD & DVD $19.95
00699492 Play Today Plus Book/CD Pack............................$14.95

Play Flute Today! DVD
00842043 Level 1 Book/CD Pack..$9.95
00842044 Level 2 Book/CD Pack..$9.95
00320360 DVD $14.95
00842045 Songbook Book/CD Pack....................................$12.95
00699553 Beginner's Pack – Level 1 Book/CD & DVD $19.95
00699489 Play Today Plus Book/CD Pack............................$14.95

Play Clarinet Today! DVD
00842046 Level 1 Book/CD Pack..$9.95
00842047 Level 2 Book/CD Pack..$9.95
00320358 DVD $14.95
00842048 Songbook Book/CD Pack....................................$12.95
00699554 Beginner's Pack – Level 1 Book/CD & DVD $19.95
00699490 Play Today Plus Book/CD Pack............................$14.95

Play Trumpet Today! DVD
00842052 Level 1 Book/CD Pack..$9.95
00842053 Level 2 Book/CD Pack..$9.95
00320357 DVD $14.95
00842054 Songbook Book/CD Pack....................................$12.95
00699556 Beginner's Pack – Level 1 Book/CD & DVD $19.95
00699491 Play Today Plus Book/CD Pack............................$14.95

Play Trombone Today! DVD
00699917 Level 1 Book/CD Pack..$9.95
00320508 DVD..$14.95

Play Violin Today!
00699748 Level 1 Book/CD Pack..$9.95

Play Recorder Today!
00700919 Level 1 Book/CD Pack..$7.95

FOR MORE INFORMATION, SEE YOUR LOCAL MUSIC DEALER, OR WRITE TO:

HAL•LEONARD® CORPORATION
7777 W. BLUEMOUND RD. P.O. BOX 13819 MILWAUKEE, WI 53213

Visit us online at **www.halleonard.com**

Prices, contents and availability subject to change without notice.

0809